For my parents, who gifted me with a love of learning and the importance of making a difference.
For the children with facial differences who inspired this story and whose courage and strength are endless.
–Marissa Suchyta, MD, PhD

To my wife Rawan, the love of my life and my partner in all my journeys—you inspire me. And to my lovely children Celine, Tarek, Rakan, and Elyana. You have filled my life with joy, happiness, and excitement. I am full of admiration for your curiosity, intelligence, and passion for life. I love you from the bottom of my heart. To my parents who instilled in me a passion to help others. I love you and appreciate you. And to the children I have had the privilege to take care of throughout my career, you have taught me bravery, kindness, graciousness, and love; you are my heroes.
–Samir Mardini, MD

We are blessed at Mayo Clinic to have a phenomenal team who brought this story of bravery, thoughtfulness, and resilience to life in a beautifully illustrated work. Thank you to our incredible partners in this journey: Dani Valladares, Jenny Krueger, Gunnar Soroos, Nina Weiner, and Dan Harke. We would like to deeply thank all the extraordinary children and families who helped us shape this story. A special thank you to Marie and Louise Harke; you helped us with this story more than you think. We appreciate you.

MAYO CLINIC PRESS KIDS | An imprint of Mayo Clinic Press
200 First St. SW, Rochester, MN 55905
mcpress.mayoclinic.org

To stay informed about Mayo Clinic Press, please subscribe to our free e-newsletter at MCPress.MayoClinic.org/parenting or follow us on social media.

The medical information in this book is true and complete to the best of our knowledge. It is not intended to replace, countermand or conflict with advice given to you by your own physician. The ultimate decision concerning your care should be made between you and your doctor. Information in this book is offered with no guarantees. The author and publisher disclaim all liability in connection with the use of this book. The views expressed are the author's personal views, and do not necessarily reflect the policy or position of Mayo Clinic.

For bulk sales contact Mayo Clinic at SpecialSalesMayoBooks@mayo.edu.

Proceeds from the sale of every book benefit important medical research and education at Mayo Clinic.

ISBN: 979-8-88770-011-3 (hardcover) | 979-8-88770-012-0 (ebook)

Library of Congress Control Number: 2023046228
Printed in China

My Extraordinary Face

Written by
Marissa Suchyta, MD, PhD
and Samir Mardini, MD

Illustrated by
Violet Tobacco

MAYO CLINIC PRESS KIDS

Every face is special.

Your face is one of a kind.

Our faces can show many wonderful feelings.

We
smile...

We
laugh...

We are **calm...**   We are **surprised!**

What are some feelings you show with your face?

No one's face
is ordinary.

Each one is **extraordinary** in its own way!

What is your favorite part of your face?

But sometimes when you're extraordinary, it isn't easy to fit in.

It can feel like you are all alone in a big world.

Have you ever felt alone?

Sometimes, people might stare.

Sometimes, they might whisper to each other.

They might have questions because there is no one else exactly like you.

You are unique.

When this happens, there's a
special trick you can use.

Gather up all
the **love** and
care and
kindness
inside you.

Let it fill your
entire chest.

Now blow it all out into an **enormous** bubble around you.

Your bubble blocks the stares.
Inside the bubble, you are powerful.

Let's practice blowing up your bubble.

Take a deep breath in

and let it all the way out.

In here, you are **safe.**

Now think about
three things that
make you proud.

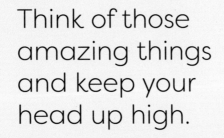

Think of those
amazing things
and keep your
head up high.

Stand up tall.

Fill your bubble
with pride.

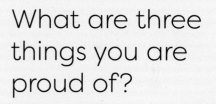

What are three
things you are
proud of?

Sometimes, people might ask you a lot of questions about what makes you extraordinary.

Part of your confidence bubble is having a plan for how to answer.

Let's create your plan.
What will you say?

Sometimes, people might try to burst your bubble.

They might say unkind things about how special you are.

When this happens, you can say "I don't need to listen to this."

You can walk away and find a friend.
Your bubble will always follow. Let's practice this.

What is a mean comment that someone has said to you before?

What would you say to them from inside your bubble?

When you talk to someone you trust, your bubble **grows...**

and grows...

and grows!

Who is someone you can talk to?

Remember, your face is one part of the **amazing** person you are.

You are **confident, special,** and **one of a kind.**

We can all smile our extraordinary smiles.

These smiles light up a world that is just as unique as you are.

A Note to Caregivers

My Extraordinary Face was written based on our experiences with children with facial differences. This book is designed to guide you and your child to build confidence, plan for encountering staring or curiosity, answer peers' questions, and develop meaningful friendships.

Marissa Suchyta, MD, PhD
Samir Mardini, MD

Be open to discussing your child's differences

If your child has a facial difference, it's important that your family talk openly about it. Even though it may feel kinder to avoid the topic, this can leave your child underprepared for questions from friends or for new social situations. More importantly, it could actually make them feel like they should be ashamed and hide their difference. We suggest making your child's unique feature a normal topic of conversation right from the start. That way, they'll grow up feeling confident and proud of who they are.

It's a good idea to talk about your child's difference just like you talk about anything else. Don't wait for them to ask—show them you're okay with how they look. This helps them feel ready to talk about it with others too. And remember, they should feel comfortable coming to you with any questions or worries they have about their facial difference or any other concerns about the way they look. Your family's openness sets the tone for how they'll feel about themselves.

Address others' natural curiosity

Let your child know that it's normal for other kids, especially younger ones, to be curious about facial differences. Some might stare or ask questions that feel unkind. But it's important to explain that it's often from a place of real interest, not unkindness.

Understanding this curiosity can boost your child's confidence. The tools in *My Extraordinary Face*, like the "bubble tool" and "confidence tool," can help them handle public stares. Practice these responses as part of a daily routine, until they feel natural. For example, your child could always blow up their confidence bubble after brushing their teeth.

Develop simple explanations with your child

Open family talks help your child discuss their facial difference. Confident responses to common questions lead to confidence when facing new situations with other children. Practice can boost your child's readiness.

Highlight their skills and the interests they share with other kids. This builds self-esteem and limits uncertainty when talking about their difference with other children. Role-play at home first, keeping answers simple and fitting their age.

Here are a few examples:

What happened to your face?
I was born this way. My head is just shaped differently from yours and my ears are a lot smaller.

This is just a very red birthmark. It's called a Port Wine Stain.

Can I catch it?
No, you can't catch it.

Does it hurt?
No, it doesn't hurt.

Did you always look this way?
Yes, I was born this way.

No, I was in an accident when I was two.

Can't doctors fix that?
I have some great doctors. They are helping me hear better.

Entering school

Start the school year by meeting with your child's teacher. This will help the teacher understand the unique challenges of having a facial difference and how to address them.

Share your child's prepared answers to questions with the teacher, so they're ready for other kids' questions.

This prepares for a smoother school year. Discuss medical needs too, and clear up any misunderstandings.

Your child might consider giving a short presentation for the class. This may sound overwhelming, but our patients have found that this is a way for the child to control the conversation around their facial difference. Your child can explain their facial difference and show photos of themselves in everyday situations. It's a chance for friendships to bloom and questions to be answered. A caregiver's presence is reassuring.

Dealing with teasing

Tell your child they can always talk to you about unkind comments. Ask them more about the comments. Stay connected to their feelings. Watch for signs and self-critical remarks such as "I hate my face."

Teach your child that people who bully often have their own insecurities. They should know they can ask for help.

When teased, encourage your child to confidently say, "I don't need to listen" and walk away calmly. Practicing other responses, like using facts, humor, or changing the topic, can help too.

Remember, teachers can be great allies. If teasing comes up, let them know. They're there to help.

Equally important, help your child build a circle of friends. Plan playdates, invite others—friendships matter. At school, these connections boost confidence.

"Your ears are funny."

Use **information:** "That's because I was born this way."

Use **humor:** "Yes, I'm really good at listening to you."

Use **distraction:** "So what? I can still play. Let's play kickball."

Meeting kids with similar experiences is wonderful too. Your child's doctors might be able to connect you with another family who understands.

Helping siblings and family members

Being the sibling of someone with a facial difference is its own challenge. Siblings might get questions about their brother or sister's appearance. Open conversations at home can help them feel ready to respond.

Invite them to join in role-playing too. It will help them handle questions from friends and peers. Plus, it will show they're a big support. As a caregiver, remember that siblings might feel caught between protecting their brother or sister and fitting in with friends. This mix of emotions is normal. Also, siblings might sometimes feel left out. Show them extra attention, understand their feelings, and make time for one-on-one moments.

It is important you have support

We understand the stress and concerns you face as a caregiver of a child with a facial difference. To care for others, you must care for yourself. Seek help when needed and build a support system.

We know it can be isolating. Educating others is important but tiring. You can politely end conversations with, "We actually need to get going." Connect with your child's medical team for support. They can link you with other understanding caregivers.

Enjoy *My Extraordinary Face* with your child. In this big world, every child deserves confidence and support. You're not alone on this journey.